"Before I could finish this book, sion executive with the words, 'I issues more urgent than how to sl fer wealth, without creating dependency. This book offers specific practical strategies, grounded in godliness."

—DR. MIRIAM ADENEY, *Associate Professor of Global and Urban Ministries, Seattle Pacific University*

"It has been said that real partnerships—whether in marriage, business or God's mission—go through at least four stages: from friendship to formation to function to fruitfulness. Daniel Rickett's excellent book on mission partnerships clearly chronicles how to avoid decisions and actions that keep partnerships from progressing through these stages. Just as important, it presents positive principles and examples about how to achieve real fruitfulness in mission partnerships for the sake of God's missionary kingdom."

—REV. B. STEVE HUGHEY, *Director, Mission Partnership & Involvement, Lutheran Church-Missouri Synod*

"It seems like everyone agrees today that ministries should function in partnerships; yet very few do. This book addresses the need in a compelling way and also provides step-by-step guidance that is invaluable in avoiding pitfalls. Everyone can benefit from the wisdom that Daniel Rickett provides."

—DR. JAMES F. ENGEL, *Founder and President Emeritus, Development Associates International*

"There was a country song that had as its title, 'I was country before country was cool'. In church and mission circles partnership is now 'cool' but Partners International was doing it long before it became cool. As with any topic which becomes 'cool,' partnership has become occluded by the fog of anecdotal experience and idealistic bias. In this little book Daniel

Rickett dissipates some of the fog and demystifies the process. He lays out clear definitions and practical 'how to's' so that you as a church or individual can benefit from true knowledge about this essential modern day tool for global ministry."

—REV. PAUL MCKAUGHAN, *President,*
Evangelical Fellowship of Mission Agencies (EFMA)

"The growing global nature of the Church makes partnership between east/west and north/south an essential part of our future. This book points to key issues that need to be considered, particularly between Western and non-Western 'partners.' You will find the check-lists particularly helpful as guidelines for planning and Kingdom action."

—MR. PHILL BUTLER, *Founder, InterDev*

UPDATED
BUILDING STRATEGIC
RELATIONSHIPS

UPDATED
BUILDING STRATEGIC
RELATIONSHIPS

*A Practical Guide to Partnering with
Non-Western Missions*

D A N I E L   R I C K E T T

PARTNERS
International

WINEPRESS WP PUBLISHING

ISBN 1-57921-449-5
LCCN: 2002101823

Dedication

To my mentor, Allen Finley
who taught me how to partner with
the servants of God in the hard places.

Content

Introduction

No mission or church can go it alone. For missions giants, mega-churches, and newcomers alike, intercultural partnerships have become central to ministry success, particularly in restricted countries like China, India, North Africa, and countries of the Middle East. More than ever, the opportunities and manpower for world evangelization lie in the hands of the Two-Thirds World Church. In this new age of missions, coalitions, alliances, and strategic partnerships are not an option; they are a necessity. To take advantage of the opportunities, and be a part of what God is doing around the world, churches and missions today must be able to create and sustain a variety of intercultural partnerships.

This book aims to help the global outreach teams of local churches to be more successful in creating and guiding their strategic relationships with non-Western missions. To that end it offers both conceptual and practical tools for assessing intercultural partnerships and building collaborative relationships that work.

"The body is a unit, though it is made up of many parts; and though all its parts are many, they form one body. . . .

Now you are the body of Christ, and each one of you is a part of it" (1 Corinthians 12:12,27).

Unlike any time in history, we have the opportunity to apply the New Testament principles of *koinonea* (fellowship) on a global scale as we build partnerships for world evangelization. We hope you will find this book a useful guide in that endeavor.

1
Defining Partnership

"Building an effective partnership."

It sounds good, but what exactly do we mean by *partnership*? To be sure we all have the same understanding, let's begin with a definition: *A partnership is a complementary relationship driven by a common purpose and sustained by a willingness to learn and grow together in obedience to God.*

With that definition in mind, let's see what it looks like in action.

A BROTHER LIKE THAT

A man came out of a store and saw a young boy hanging around his new car. Suspicious of the boy he asked, "What are you doing?"

"Studying this car," the boy replied.

Yeah, sure, the man thought. So he began to quiz the boy. "What kind of car is it?" he asked.

"A 1999 Mercedes Benz."

"What color?"

"Metallic burgundy."

After a few more questions, the man realized the little guy knew what he was talking about, and they began to chat. The boy asked how much he paid for the car. The man replied, "Nothing. I had a need and my brother gave it to me."

"I wish . . . ," the boy started.

". . . that you had a brother like that?" the man interrupted.

"No," said the boy. "I wish I could *be* a brother like that."

For those of us who partner with indigenous ministries, our driving passion is "to be a brother like that." We strive to help the servants of God around the world so they can be free to build the Church of Jesus Christ in the least Christian regions of the world.

True partnership can be summed up in one word: *brotherhood*. If we can achieve genuine brotherhood, we can succeed at partnership. But while brotherhood is both a consequence of our identity in Christ and an expression of Christian love, it doesn't come easily. In today's global village we have to learn how to deal with each other as true brothers and sisters, while also learning to obey God and advance the gospel. That is quite a charge! And ultimately it brings us to very practical questions about sharing power, resources, and responsibilities.

PARTNERSHIP IS RISKY

The story of the boy and the Mercedes Benz epitomizes what we all wish we could do for our brothers and sisters in the hard places of the world. If it is in our power to give what our brother or sister needs, we will happily give it for the sake of the gospel. But the story also triggers some disturbing questions.

What makes me think my brother needs a Mercedes Benz? Do I know what he needs because he asked me? Or do I give a Mercedes because *I* think that's what he needs? Suppose my brother is making $20,000 a year. How is he going to afford the maintenance on a $60,000 Mercedes? My intention is to be generous, but my generosity becomes his burden.

To have something to share is a wonderful thing. To give your brother what he needs when he needs it is even better. But because what is needed is not always apparent, giving can be a dangerous business.

Those of us who partner with indigenous ministries face a subtle and constant danger. It's not primarily dependency, although that is the risk for which we are most often criticized. Nor is it paternalism, although we do slip into that more often than we care to admit. No, it is something harder to deal with than either of these.

THE MOST CHALLENGING QUESTION

The most challenging question is this: *Have we contributed to the self-developing capabilities of our partners?* The surest way to prevent dependency is to pay close attention to development. It is also the best safeguard against paternalism. *By focusing on development, we are forced to ask whether our involvement makes our brothers and sisters better able to serve God according to their own gifts and calling.* Are we helping to build their capacity or are we simply relieving their needs?

SO WHAT IS GOOD PARTNERSHIP?

The most enduring partnerships are complementary. *A complementary partnership is the association of two or more autonomous bodies who have formed a trusting relationship and fulfill agreed-upon expectations. They do this by sharing complementary gifts and abilities in order to achieve a common goal.* A complementary partnership, then, is a relationship of shared commitment and interdependency.

A complementary partnership requires at least three prerequisites:

One, partnering organizations must be independent of one another. Before entering into the partnership each ministry must have its own separate identity and government. Independence is a prerequisite for interdependence. Consider, for instance, the differences between the partnering relationship of a sending mission to a daughter church, and one between two previously independent organizations. The former must first work through a process of separation and independence before it can move toward interdependence. The latter, on the other hand, can start with an assumption of interdependence.

Two, there must be compatibility in doctrinal beliefs and ministry values. This prerequisite usually takes care of itself. Rarely will people from significantly different theological persuasions establish an intimate alliance. But there must also be a fit in the priorities of ministry. If, for example, one partner emphasizes holistic ministry, that should be more than a passing interest to the other partner. If it isn't, there will soon be conflict.

Three, each partner must know and be willing to exchange complementary strengths and resources. Unless each partner has something the other needs, there is nothing to be exchanged. Organizations form partnerships precisely because they lack something others can offer. This is where the strength of one makes up for the weakness of the other, enabling partners to leverage their respective capabilities, resources, and opportunities. A partnership that does not significantly benefit each partner will not endure.

WHAT IS DEVELOPMENT?

Development is what happens when people learn, grow, and change. It is at once a *process* and a *result*. It is a process because people are learning, taking charge of their own lives, and solving their own problems. It is a result when people actually change the conditions of life.

As Christians, we believe the *means* to development is faith in Christ. The *end* of development is a life of faithfulness to Him. The *process* is growing in Christ and as responsible stewards. The *result* is people living out Kingdom values and putting God on display.

This view of development is fixed in the belief that growth occurs as people examine their own problems in the light of Scripture. They identify solutions that involve gaining new knowledge and skills, which are then translated into appropriate actions.

In the final analysis, *development is that which people do for themselves.* It cannot be imposed from the outside. No one can make another person develop any more than a farmer can make a plant grow. A plant grows according to its own internal code. The farmer's task is to work with the plant, to add water and fertilizer, and to keep the weeds away. But it is God who makes the plant grow. In the same way one person can only help another person along. Development is the responsibility of the individual, or in the case of an organization, of those who share in the risks and rewards of the ministry. In the end, it is always God who brings the increase.

WHAT IS A DEVELOPMENTAL PARTNERSHIP?

If development is growth in self-developing capabilities, and partnership is the mutual sharing of resources for a common goal, then *a developmental partnership in Christian ministry is a cooperative relationship between two autonomous bodies whereby each enables the other to grow in its capacity to initiate and carry out change for the sake of the gospel.* What makes a partnership distinctly developmental is a conscious effort to strengthen the self-developing capabilities of the organization.

Although no two partnerships are exactly the same, developmental partnerships have three characteristics in common: results, relationship, and vision.

Results *describe a partnership's capacity to deliver tangible outcomes.* The ministry should emerge from an alliance stronger and more effective than it was when it entered. No matter how cozy or friendly a relationship may be, its purpose is to accomplish something in the ministry of the gospel. Whether it is to plant churches among unreached peoples, to empower disenfranchised Christians, to equip leaders for ministry, or to carry out acts of mercy for the poor, every successful partnership has results as its reason for being. The hallmark of developmental partnering is that it creates results both in ministry and in each organization's ability to learn, change, and grow.

Relationship *is the means by which trust, communication, and collaboration are made possible.* Developmental partnerships move far beyond transactional relationships and achieve a deep sense of kinship.

In a transactional relationship a single representative from each organization works out an agreement. The relationship is managed largely through those two points of contact. Developmental partnering involves a whole new level of relationship. Rather than limiting the points of contact, it involves multiple contacts at many different levels of the organization.

This doesn't mean merely bringing more people into the process. Development requires broad representation of the capabilities within each organization. Different parts of each become resources to the other in the learning process. Accordingly, communication channels tend to be informal and spontaneous. (Tightly structured channels inhibit learning and change.)

Of course, communication is only as rich as trust is deep. Closer contact and higher levels of interaction are important ingredients for building understanding and trust. This too is a function of breadth—the right people talking with one another about the shared responsibility of development. Yet, developmental partnering is more than the establishment of relationships between two ministries. "A healthy, mature relationship between churches," writes G. Thompson Brown, "may be a prerequisite for mission, but it can never take its place."

He continues:

> The church must be seen as the base from which mission moves out into the world. Churches enter into partnership, not so much to help each other, although this may be a by-product of mission, but to share resources, insights and spiritual gifts in the crossing of frontiers, in bearing witness of a common faith to an unbelieving world, and in demonstrating by deeds of compassion and justice God's love for his suffering and alienated creation.[1]

Relationship, no matter how enriching, is not enough to sustain a developmental partnership. That's because a relationship does not, on its own, produce results. It simply makes results possible. If you have no vision of what those results should be, or no way to make them happen, you will not realize the full advantage of partnering in missions.

Vision is a compelling picture of what the partnership can achieve and how it is going to get there. Developmental partnerships have a shared road map that helps them set expectations, measure progress, and maximize the value of collaboration.

The vision is what gives the ministry an incentive to partner. It shows how the partners together can be more than the sum of their parts.

Developmental partnering is only possible where the overall development of the ministry is in view, where openness, caring and mutual support mark the relationship, and where sustainable strength and value are added to the ministry.

CAN WE ACT LIKE BROTHERS?

Developmental partnering helps a ministry grow in its capacity to create and manage change in obedience to God. Realizing that people are authors of their own development, we cannot presume to show the way. All we can do is help them find their own way to become biblically faithful and effective missionaries. Our job is to enhance the skills of local Christian leaders in releasing the creative potential and indigenous resources of the people of God. To do so requires that we come alongside ministry leaders, listen and respond to *their* agenda, and together find ways to help it result in the growth and success of their ministry.

Developmental partnering is the practice of brotherhood. If we can achieve true brotherhood, we will in a single stroke enrich one another and advance the gospel. But there is no formula for the practice of genuine brotherhood. It requires constant attention, open communication, mutual support, prayer, persistence, and heavy doses of forgiveness all around.

READINESS CHECKLIST
Ten Things to Consider Before Forming a Partnership

	Current Status			Action (When & Whom)
	Have it	Don't have it	Needs work	
1. Do we have a clear understanding of the potential partner's ministry?				
2. Does the potential partner have a track record of fruitful ministry?				
3. Is the potential partner autonomous and capable of standing on its own?				
4. Do we have compatibility in doctrinal beliefs and ministry priorities?				
5. Can we envision goals that would satisfy important values on both sides of the partnership?				
6. Do we have a clear sense of what each partner would bring to the relationship?				
7. Do we feel that the conditions are right for partnership?				

	Have it	Current Status Don't have it	Needs work	Action (When & Whom)
8. Are key personnel in each ministry prepared to champion the partnership?				
9. Can we define clear mutual expectations about how we will work together?				
10. Can we put adequate systems in place to measure and track progress?				

2
Understanding Dependency

The loudest objection to partnership with non-Western missions is the fear that it will create dependency. We seem to assume that it is better to leave our brothers and sisters in Christ alone than to run the risk of making them dependent. But as Chuck Bennett points out: "To refuse to share our resources with overseas brethren because there have been abuses is like saying we should outlaw marriage because some husbands beat their wives. The problem is real but the solution is simplistic."[1]

The issue of dependency in mission relationships is widely recognized. What is often overlooked is that there are two kinds of dependency: healthy and unhealthy. If there is to be a productive partnership, it is crucial that we understand the difference between the two. Only then can we develop ways to use it constructively.

DEPENDENCY DEFINED

Dependency is the state of relying on someone or something. To be dependent is, first and foremost, to be reliant on another.

Reliance can actually be more important than being independent. The fact is that no one can go it alone. In many ways, every one of us depends on a wide variety of people and institutions. Pastors depend on parishioners, missionaries depend on donors, organizations depend on employees, universities depend on students.

Certainly it is possible to rely too heavily on someone or something. When medical patients become habituated to drugs we call it dependency. When people remain on government welfare for a lifetime we call it dependency. When an adult child remains too long with his parents we call it dependency. Yet when a missionary receives all of his or her support from a few churches, we *don't* call it dependency. When a mission agency relies exclusively on a single association of churches, we don't call that dependency either. Although every church and mission is sustained by multi-lateral dependencies, we don't think of them as being dependent.

So what makes a certain kind of dependency acceptable and another kind unacceptable? Why is it that a dependent child is legitimate but a dependent adult is not? The answer lies in the dependent's willingness and capacity to do his or her part—that is, to take responsibility and give something back. Although we are all dependent in countless ways, dependency goes over the line when people fail to take responsibility where they can.

DEPENDENCY IN THE BODY OF CHRIST

Perhaps the first thing to understand is where dependency fits into the Christian context. The biblical view of the Church is that it is one body made up of many parts (1 Corinthians 12:12–27). In this body, God distributes spiritual gifts for the building up the Church and putting Christ on display. The nature of the Church is such that as each part does its work, the entire body grows in Christ (Ephesians 4:1–16). Is it not outrageous for the eyes to tell the hands that they have no need of them? Or the feet to tell the ears they are of no use?

If Christians are to avoid dependency, what are we to do with the command to carry one another's burdens and so fulfill the law of Christ (Galatians 6:2)? What are we to say when we see our brother in need and have the means to help (1 John 3:16–20)? And what are we to make of Paul's collection of funds from the churches of Asia Minor for the suffering church in Jerusalem (1 Corinthians 16:1–3)?

Rather than steer Christians away from reliance on one another, the Bible seems to celebrate dependency in the body of Christ. Yet this is clearly *not* the way we normally think of dependency. The dependency implied by the image of the body is *complimentary* and *reciprocal*. One part of the body cannot deny another part without in some way denying itself. All the parts of the body are knit together in such a way that every part has something to give and something to receive. Perhaps this is why the New Testament authors so often remind us of our oneness in Christ. Christians are designed for each other as well as for Christ.

It is important to note that, as with all analogies, at some point the comparison of the human body with the spiritual body of Christ breaks down. The parts of the human body are obviously mutually dependent. But mutuality among Christians does not happen so automatically. It requires a conscious effort. Such dependency demands regard for the commands of Scripture and cooperation with the Holy Spirit. The declaration of the Bible that the body of Christ is one must be balanced with the demands found in the Bible. All of the instruction about how to do good and relate to one another

as members of Christ's body are expected from and commanded of all believers. For example, believers are declared
one in Christ, yet they are commanded to be like-minded, to
love one another, and to work together with one heart and
purpose (Romans 12:4–8, Philippians 2:1–2). In Christ there
is no racial or cultural distinction, yet Christians are commanded to keep the unity of the Spirit through the bond of
peace (1 Corinthians 12:13, Ephesians 2:14–16, 4:3). The Holy
Spirit administers spiritual gifts as He sees fit, yet believers
are commanded to use their gifts for the common good (1
Corinthians 12:1–11, 1 Peter 4:10–11). No part of the body
of Christ can cease to be part of the whole, yet all believers
are admonished to have equal concern for each other, to share
in one another's sufferings and rejoice in one another's victo-
ries (1 Corinthians 12:14–26).

Clearly, then, dependency in the body of Christ is not *pas-
sive* but very *active*. It demands that Christians take up their
responsibilities in the body. Such commands as to share with
one another (Romans 12:13), care for one another (Galatians
6:2), support one another's interests (Philippians 2:4), and
serve one another (1 Peter 4:10) all require responsible action. The command to do good, especially to the family of
believers, is given to those who receive as well as those who
give (Galatians 6:10). No Christian—whether rich or poor,
young or old, weak or strong—is exempt from taking responsibility. That's because responsibility makes reciprocity both
possible and dependency beneficial.

HEALTHY DEPENDENCY

Taking our cues from the Bible, the kind of dependency
expected from and commanded of Christians is characterized
by reciprocity and responsibility. Thus, in a healthy relationship both partners recognize their responsibilities and work
to fulfill them. Each enters the relationship with a clear pic-

ture of what each has to offer and what each stands to gain. Each maintains its independence and capacity to instruct, correct, and refuse the other. Each honors and upholds the unique and divine calling of the other. Each makes a distinctive and complementary contribution to the partnership. Each conducts itself in a manner that safeguards one another's integrity and honors Christ. Therefore, it is important in a partnership to not only give but to receive, to not only teach but to learn, and to not only lead but to follow. By contrast, the seeds of unhealthy dependency are planted when the only deal struck in a mission relationship is the one-way flow of resources, whether that be money or personnel.

UNHEALTHY DEPENDENCY

Unhealthy dependency occurs when reciprocity and responsibility are ignored, overruled, or undervalued. If the accent is on the exchange of money or personnel and not on the complementary contributions each partner makes, the importance of reciprocity is easily overlooked. If resources are shared more for the benefit of one partner than for the purpose of ministering more effectively to others, the receiving partner's responsibility is effectively sidelined. If one partner maintains control over the decision-making process, the other partner cannot exercise responsibility as a co-laborer. If one partner's contributions are valued more highly than the others', it is impossible to establish true reciprocity. In the end, if a partnership is not joining in a common purpose and sharing complementary resources, it cannot be reciprocal and it will not be responsible.

Five Sure Ways to Create Unhealthy Dependency

Several factors may coalesce into unhealthy dependency, but there are five starting points that almost guarantee it.

Make an alliance with a lone ranger. An independent ministry leader may be the next John Wesley, or he may be a very talented individual with a self-serving agenda. Unless you've known the individual for some time, it's difficult to discern real intentions. Bogus, questionable organizations that compete for mission dollars tend to by-pass local churches. If you're not working with a ministry that has a local board of directors or the equivalent, there's a chance you've been found by a fortune hunter.

Send money directly to individuals. Unless individuals are employees or contract laborers with whom you have a performance agreement and means of accountability, sending funds directly can put people in a precarious position. Individuals cannot vouch for themselves; they need others to verify their testimony. Even the Apostle Paul was not willing to convey funds without the involvement of trusted men from the contributing churches (1 Corinthians 16:3, 2 Corinthians 8:16–21). It takes a bona fide organization with a governing structure and accounting system to administer funds in an auditable and defensible manner.

Finance pastors and local churches. History has shown that foreign funding of pastors and churches has proven more often than not to hinder genuine indigenous growth. Foreign funding can easily stifle local initiative by creating the assumption that believers need only rely on distant benefactors rather than learn to give sacrificially. It can cause pastors to become preoccupied with raising foreign funds, and fail to be creative in maximizing local resources. Foreign funding of some pastors and not others creates jealousies, and frees them from accountability to the local Christian community. In the matter of funding pastors, the chances of creating unhealthy dependency are at their highest.

Give resources based only on need. A partnership that sets out to satisfy needs soon finds itself running a race with no end. That's because needs alone are insatiable. Giving based solely on need creates a pipeline of supply that in turn raises the expectation of future need satisfaction. Needs have to be defined and boundaries set so that you can actually see results. At a minimum, giving should be based on what will enhance

- responsibility—each partner's ability to meet their obligations as Christians,

- reciprocity—each partner's ability to make distinctive and complementary contributions, and

- results—the ability to achieve specific ministry outcomes.

Underwrite 100% of a ministry's need. Money is one form of power, and in international partnerships it has proven to be the most problematic. When one ministry relies solely on another for financial support, the balance of power leans heavily toward the funding source. This is a problem because unhealthy dependency thrives on the imbalance of power. The best antidote is to subsidize a strategic initiative or program rather than to fund the entire ministry.

There is a sixth way to create unhealthy dependency. It's not listed above because it teeters on the border between acceptable and unacceptable dependency. It's the hiring of local Christians to run Western programs. Unless you plan to establish a local branch of your church or mission, hiring local people can be the first step to unhealthy dependency. The reason is simple: *hiring local Christians is not partnership; it's employment.* There may be very good reasons to hire local people to administer programs of a foreign mission. But employment relationships should never be confused with partnership. When a Western agency hires local people, they assume all the responsibilities of an employer: fair and competitive wages, medical insurance, retirement benefits, direct management of performance, and compliance with local labor laws. Even then, Western employers have to cope with the potential of providing their employees with lifestyles far above their peers, making it possible for them to bypass local Christian authority, and creating jealousies locally and internationally.

Managing Dependency: A Few Don'ts

If a healthy dependency is to be preserved, there are certain things partners in the work of the gospel should never do to each other. Here are seven taboos that must be observed:

They don't define goals and methods unilaterally. For Western partners especially this means don't assume you know what the task is and what the goals are. Don't first develop a plan, then merely invite non-Western partners to join in at a later stage. If you really want a partnership, ask your partners what God is inviting them to do, then build a plan together to achieve it.

They don't base the relationship on a one-way flow of resources. Complementarity, not assistance, lies at the heart of effective partnerships. *Assistance* is focused on meeting the needs and interests of one party. *Complementarity* concerns the accomplishment of mutual purposes and a shared vision, and includes each partner's needs and interests. A partnership moves beyond assistance to complementarity when each partner makes different but crucial contributions to a common goal.

They don't allow money to become the most highly valued resource. In the affluent West, where ministries rely on capital-intensive and technology-intensive strategies, making the claim that money will not be the driving force is fine in principle but difficult in practice. Unfortunately, this difficulty spills over into mission partnerships. We tend to put a premium on our own resources rather than on the resources of our non-Western counterparts. In most cases, non-Western partners may rely on Western partners for financial and technological resources, but Western partners are dependent on the human resources, linguistic skills, cultural insight, and relevant lifestyle of its non-Western partners. Who can estimate the value of such resources? If money becomes the driving force, the golden rule takes hold—the one with the gold rules. When that happens, reciprocity is broken and shared responsibility gives way to unbalanced control.

They don't fund the full cost of a project without clear justification. In the face of enormous economic inequities, there is inherent pressure on Western partners to be the "sugar daddy" of more "needy" partners. Favorable exchange rates and the relative access to money might make it easy to underwrite projects, but it doesn't make it right. Healthy dependency flourishes on the foundation of shared responsibility. Funding decisions should be based as much on what fosters responsibility and reciprocity as on what might be accomplished. Matching grants, capital funds, one-time projects, and partial support are useful methods of shared responsibility.

They don't interfere in the administration of the partner's organization. It's one thing to give advise when you're asked for it, or even to admonish a partner in the case of serious misconduct. It's quite another thing to meddle in the internal affairs of the partner ministry. For example, Western agencies that provide support for workers tend to assume responsibility for deciding how much non-Western personnel get paid.

But this is an area that should be clearly under the control of the local authority structure.

They don't do for others what they can better do for themselves. Doing so has two serious negative consequences. One, it retards the chances of growth and development. Organizations, like people, become strong and effective only when they make decisions, initiate action, and solve problems. Two, it lowers the ceiling on what you can accomplish. Mission partners must develop the right mix of contributions, that is, each of the complementary skills, knowledge, and resources necessary to accomplish the shared vision.

They don't rely on "one-size-fits-all" policies. Policies can make decisions easier, but they can also lead to bad decisions. For example, one mission agency tries to avoid unhealthy dependency by giving only very small amounts, such as 10% of the total need. That may be fine in some situations, but it is harmful in others. A better approach is to find out what is at stake, identify what is missing, and then to determine the best contribution you can make under the circumstances.

For some, dependency in mission relationships is regarded as a condition to be avoided rather than an essential quality. But for today's missions that are assessing the missing links in their ministry capacities and seeking collaboration with non-Western missions as peers, dependency is no longer a one-sided issue. It is the key to interdependence and mutuality.

DEPENDENCY CHECKLIST
Eight Ways to Inhibit Unhealthy Dependency

	Current Status			Action (When & Whom)
	Have it	Don't have it	Needs work	
1. Do we have a clear position on dependency?				
2. Have we discussed dependency with our partners?				
3. Can we spot the signs of unhealthy dependency?				
4. Are the lines blurred between who is the beneficiary and who the benefactor?				
5. Do our partners use methods that put a Premium on local resources?				
6. Do funding decisions account for dependency?				
7. Is the relationship reciprocal?				
8. Does each partner make different but complementary contributions?				

3
Sharing Resources

Six years ago I walked with my friend David Kitonga through the mud streets of a slum outside Nairobi, Kenya. Children clambered on garbage heaps foraging for food. Sewage collected in open ditches with dozens of children crowded around. "These children are so quiet and well behaved," someone commented.

"They are quiet because they are sick," David said.

As we moved forward toward rows and rows of dark, clapboard shacks, several men hurried toward us. They were not there to greet us; they came to chase us away. The economy of that slum was based on prostitution and the production of illegal liquor. Even the police seldom ventured there.

Today in the heart of that slum stands the Huduma Church, a congregation of 300 adults and countless children. Drunkards, drug dealers, and prostitutes have come to Christ. Men are learning basic carpentry and women are trained in sewing. Children are fed once a week and given basic education. Many other programs are underway to grow the church and help the slum dwellers escape the grip of poverty.

Huduma Church is a tree of life in a field of despair. It exists, first, because local Christians had the compassion to work in the slum and, second, because a few outsiders had the humility to follow their lead.

Would the Huduma Church have come to life without outside support? I don't know. Perhaps not. But of this I am certain: the people of God are designed for each other, and the Kingdom of God advances when we work together. *The human body has many parts, but the many parts make up only one body. So it is with the body of Christ . . . Now all of you together are Christ's body, and each one of you is a separate and necessary part of it* (1 Corinthians 12:12,27, NLT). *Under his direction, the whole body is fitted together perfectly. As each part does its own special work, it helps the other parts grow, so that the whole body grows and builds itself up in love* (Ephesians 4:16, NLT).

How do we go about sharing financial resources in the work of the gospel? Advising someone on the use of money in such an endeavor is like forecasting the weather. It is a huge challenge. Both are affected by several factors that do not always behave the same way. The best we can do is to advise one another about biblical principles and general patterns of success and failure.

NAVIGATE BY BIBLICAL PRINCIPLES

Should Christians share resources in the global community of Christ? Absolutely! The Bible is very clear about how Christians are to care for one another. The Apostle Paul encouraged the Galatians to *do good to everyone, especially to our Christian brothers and sisters* (6:10, NLT). This was not merely a nice sentiment. It took Paul nearly ten years to organize a large collection of funds from the Greco-Roman cities he evangelized to be sent back to Jerusalem. The event reveals many important principles for sharing resources in the Body of Christ (Acts 21:17–19; 24:17; 2 Corinthians 8–9).

The Apostle John wrote, *But if one of you has enough money to live well, and sees a brother or sister in need and refuses to help—how can God's love be in that person* (1 John 3:17–18, NLT)? If a person who has the ability to help and is aware of acute human need—particularly within the Christian community—yet refuses to act in any way, the love of God simply cannot be in that person. Sound harsh? If these passages are not enough to guide us, there is much more in the Scriptures.

The following charts identify twenty principles that can help us think biblically about the giving and receiving of money. These are organized into two lists: Ten Laws of Receiving, and Ten Laws of Giving. Admittedly, these lists are far from complete. For a comprehensive study I recommend Craig Blomberg's book, *Neither Poverty Nor Riches: A Biblical Theology of Material Possessions.*[1]

In these lists you will find a tension between generosity and responsibility, between what we should do for others and what they should do for themselves. This is epitomized in Galatians 6. On the one hand, believers are admonished to *carry each other's burdens* (vs. 2). On the other hand, it is said that *each one should carry his own load* (vs. 5). But don't be too quick to assume it is a contradiction. Rather, it intentionally sets up the tension between doing for others and others doing for themselves. Those who would share resources in the work of the gospel must learn to navigate between the need to care for others and the need of others to care for themselves.

TEN LAWS OF RECEIVING

General Principle	Key Text
1. It is better to trust in God than in money.	Psalm 34:9–10; 107:9; 111:5; 127:2; Matthew 6:24; Hebrews 13:5
2. It is more blessed to give than to receive.	Acts 20:34–35
3. Christians are to work to provide for themselves and their families and to have something to share.	Ephesians 4:28; 1 Thessalonians 4:11–12; 1 Timothy 5:8
4. Christians are to manage their resources as stewards of what belongs to God.	Psalm 24:1–2; Matthew 25:14–30; Luke 12:48; 14:28–30; 16:10–12; Acts 17:24–28; Romans 14:12; 1 Corinthians 4:2; 2 Corinthians 5:9–10; 1 Peter 4:10
5. Christian workers have the right of support.	1 Corinthians 9:3–14; 1 Timothy 5:18
6. Christian workers should be grateful for financial support but not depend on it.	Acts 18:3; 20:33–35; 1 Corinthians 9:15–18; 2 Corinthians 11:7–10; 1 Thessalonians 2:7–9;
7. It is important not only to keep financial integrity before God but also to be perceived as doing so by others.	2 Thessalonians 3:6–9 Deuteronomy 25:13–15; 2 Corinthians 8:16–24
8. Christians can be content and thankful for God's supply.	Philippians 4:10–19
9. Some Christians may be more impoverished than others, but that gives them no right to be idle and to depend solely on "welfare" from others.	1 Thessalonians 5:14; 2 Thessalonians 3:6–15; Titus 3:14
10. Improper motives for getting money can lead to all sorts of trouble.	1 Timothy 6:9–10

TEN LAWS OF GIVING

General Principle	Key Text
1. The Lord honors the generous and withholds from the miserly.	Deuteronomy 15:10–11; Proverbs 19:17; 22:9; Isaiah 58:7, 10–11
2. Christians should beware of giving with mixed motives.	Luke 14:12–14
3. Christians should give according to what they have, not according to what they do not have.	2 Corinthians 8:12
4. The surplus that some Christians have should be used to make up for the deficiency of others.	2 Corinthians 8:13–15
5. Whoever sows generously will also reap generously.	2 Corinthians 9:6–11
6. Christians are to do good to all people, especially to fellow believers.	Galatians 6:10
7. Christians are to have Christ's attitude of self-sacrificing humility and love for others.	Philippians 2:1–5
8. Inappropriate giving can excuse others from taking responsibility.	1 Timothy 5:4, 8, 11–13, 16
9. Christians should beware of favoritism in their giving.	James 2:1–10
10. Love demands that a Christian never deny a brother in need when it is in his power to help.	1 John 3:16–20

As you can see, the giving and receiving of money in ministry is full of hazards. Ignore the tension between generosity and responsibility and there will be problems. Allow the Holy Spirit's control to be replaced by pride, selfish ambition, or greed, and there will be still more problems. The sweep of Scripture suggests that if we err let us err on the side of generosity. Let it be said that we are too loving, not controlling; too generous, not stingy; too sacrificial, not self-serving. Let it be said by the people around us, "Look how they love one another."

LEARN FROM HISTORY AND EXPERIENCE

Should local ministry be funded from the outside? History and experience answer with a definite maybe. In some cases it might be the right thing to do. In other cases it might be the wrong thing to do. There is no formula that will work in every situation. One thing is clear: giving and receiving foreign funds in the work of the gospel requires careful attention and much prayer.

In Indonesia
When churches began to spring up among the Dani people of Irian Jaya Indonesia, missionaries John and Helen Dekker were careful to encourage biblical stewardship and the use of local resources. Although the Dani still lived in the stone age and had no "money" except small sea shells, they supported their own pastors and sent dozens of missionaries to neighboring tribes. It was not until the churches had become well established that outside funds were used to help students going to Java for seminary education.

In Brazil
When Jim Orr and Marcio Garcia began to reach out to the isolated villages along the coastline of Brazil, few Brazilians

were willing to support their ministry. In the early days Partners International provided 80 percent of their entire support. Today they receive 20 percent from Partners and 80 percent from Brazilian churches. Because of this partnership more than 4,500 people confessed Christ, and 100 churches were established.

In South Africa

When Richard Makuyane began to preach on the street corners and at the bus stops of South Africa, he was completely alone. Richard had no church or mission to support him and he was constantly limited by apartheid government policies. To support his ministry he kept a small kiosk where he sold food and household items. His wife Setty worked as a nurse in a local hospital. Although Richard was barely able to read, he began winning many people to Christ. When the crowds got too large for street corners, he borrowed an old tent and continued preaching. When the tent wore out, Partners International purchased two large preaching tents. Since Richard preaches mostly to very poor people, he and Setty teach a variety of self-help skills. Although Richard and Setty work to pay their own expenses, Partners International gave them funds for their feeding programs, health clinics, literacy programs and water development projects in remote villages. Through Richard's ministry more than 10,000 people have become believers and 16 churches have been started.

In India

When God began to move among the Khond people of India, Southern Baptist missionary Calvin Fox recognized it as a spontaneous expansion of the church. He knew it was not something the missionaries had caused, nor was it something they were required to control. But they were responsible to nurture it. They did this by providing training in discipleship and in agricultural self-help. Since the Khond people are among the poorest of the poor, the mission subsidized the school for master trainers and radio programs that teach both farming techniques and Scriptures. For the Khond, the cost for those would be insurmountable, but for the mission it is very little—just $33 per Khond church per year! Today there are some 900 Khond churches and over 100,000 believers.

Although each story is different, involving different people in different parts of the world, there are definite similarities. First, the churches did not receive direct outside subsidy, nor were the pastors paid with outside funds. This is a well-established principle of church growth.[2] The healthiest churches grow out of their own indigenous resources. That does not rule out all forms of outside support, however. The Khond churches were aided in leadership training and agricultural development. Dani churches received help in training their top leaders. South African churches were assisted with a variety of self-help programs. Second, missionary work by definition requires outside support. Marcio Garcia's church planting ministry still requires outside support, though now it comes from churches within Brazil. Richard Makunyane's evangelistic ministry was similar although he accepted help with major capital expenses and specialized development projects. Third, in every case outside support came only by invitation and after careful assessment of the impact it might have.

Because there is no formula for the effective sharing of resources across national, cultural, and organizational boundaries, each new situation requires individual judgment and discernment. But much like the stars help the navigator steer a ship, there are biblical principles and lessons learned from experience to guide us.

Know the Warning Signs

When is it wrong for outsiders to fund local ministry? If you answer, "No, we don't have it" to any question in the Assessment Checklist, it may well indicate a problem. If your answer is "No, we don't have it" to more than one, it is a distinct possibility. If your answers to several questions are in the negative, it is almost certainly wrong to fund the project at this time.

To evaluate a particular situation, work through the Assessment Checklists at the end of this chapter. Have the local ministry work through Checklist A, and you, as the outside agency, work through Checklist B.

Did you spot some potential problems? Some uncertainties, perhaps? Then you have more work to do. Search for a culturally appropriate way to address those troublesome issues.

The giving and receiving of money in missions partnerships requires judgment in changing circumstances. Yet there are constants, such as the doctrine of love, the unity of all believers, the fact that we are members of the same household of God and of the one Body of Christ, and that we share a common call to glorify God and make him known.

In Christ we have all we need to build relationships of mutual respect and trust. The Body of Christ is designed so that each part has something to give to and something to receive from others. When we respect the giftedness of each part and the responsibility of every believer to steward what God has given, we will have partnerships that are complementary and mutually beneficial. Together we will proclaim Christ, grow in faith, and show the world the God we serve.

SERVE ONE ANOTHER

I will long remember the first global conference hosted by Partners International. It was 1987, the week following the ground breaking COMIBAM conference in Sao Paulo, Brazil.[3] Ministry leaders gathered from all over the world to discuss the nuts and bolts of partnership. The most enduring result of the meeting was a covenant drafted by the leaders of partner ministries. The purpose of the statement was to establish the common ground on which our partnerships would stand. Here is what they said:

As those who share in God's grace with each other (Philippians 1:7), who have been qualified to share in the inheritance of the saints in the kingdom of light (Colossians 1:12), who share in the heavenly calling (Hebrews 3:1), who share in his holiness (Hebrews 12:10), and who will share in the glory to be revealed (1 Peter 5:1), we as partners in the work of God affirm:

1. We are called to invest our lives and resources in Christ's ministry of reconciliation (2 Corinthians 5:18);
2. God has given his church a variety of gifts to complement each other in the ministry of equipping it to fulfill its mandate for the glory of Christ (Ephesians 4:11–13);
3. In seeking to fulfill this mandate, we recognize that our ability does not depend on human criteria such as wealth, education, experience, and so on, but on the Holy Spirit (Zechariah 4:6);
4. It is both an honor and an obligation for Christians to assist one another in the work of Christ (2 Corinthians 8:1–15);
5. Any God-honoring service should be carried out in a spirit of mutual respect, trust and submission in the Lord (Colossians 3:23–24; Galatians 5:13);
6. Mutual accountability is an integral aspect of Christian stewardship (1 Corinthians 4:2; Romans 14:12); and
7. Our motivation should be that of a servant in keeping with the example of Christ (Philippians 2:1–11).

If we are to be the people of God in the global neighborhood, let us resolve to bathe our partnering relationships in prayer, and to reflect together on our standing in Christ. Let us commit to our mutual call to the work of the gospel, all the while *agreeing wholeheartedly with each other, loving one another, and working together with one heart and purpose* (Philippians 2:2, NLT).

Only then will we gain the discernment and courage to act like true brothers and sisters in Christ.

ASSESSMENT CHECKLIST A
Ten Signs of Effective Resource Sharing

Local Ministry	Current Status			Action (When & Whom)
	Have it	Don't have it	Needs work	
1. Does the outside agency avoid setting up programs without first consulting with the local Christian community?				
2. Does the outsider inquire of local Christian leaders about what needs to be done?				
3. Is the outsider guarded about the use of strategies that depend upon expensive technology that is otherwise beyond the capacity of local ministries?				
4. Is the outsider cautious about the possible negative effects of his relative affluence on the communication of the gospel?				
5. Does the outsider avoid exploiting the local situation to promote his or her own ministry?				

	Current Status			Action (When & Whom)
Local Ministry	Have it	Don't have it	Needs work	
6. Does the outsider launch funding programs only after establishing the trustworthiness of a local ministry to receive and handle outside funds?				
7. Is the outsider keenly aware that outside support can potentially destroy the selfhood of the recipients?				
8. Is the outsider aware of how foreign support may dampen reliance on local funding?				
9. Does the outsider avoid recruiting local Christians and paying them salaries far above local standards?				
10. Does the outsider guard against taking on so many projects that he cannot provide satisfactory attention and accountability to this one?				

ASSESSMENT CHECKLIST B
Ten Signs of Effective Resource Sharing

		Current Status		Action (When & Whom)
Outside Agency	Have it	Don't have it	Needs work	
1. Are local Christian leaders generally in favor of the idea?				
2. Does the outside support enhance the recipient's capacity to make its own decisions and chart its own course?				
3. Does the outside support in no way limit the recipient's ability to collaborate with other local Christian communities?				
4. Does the outside support enhance the recipients' sense of selfhood and dignity as co-laborers in the work of the gospel?				
5. Does the recipient ministry reflect dependence upon God and not money as the source of ministry success?				

	Current Status			Action (When & Whom)
Outside Agency	Have it	Don't have it	Needs work	
6. Is the proportion of outside support well below the level of support from within the region?				
7. Does the recipient ministry avoid partiality in its stewardship of outside support? Does it avoid showing favoritism to ethnic groups, churches, or individuals?				
8. Does the alliance implied by the outside support in no way alienate Christians from their local community?				
9. Does the recipient insist on sending money to the overseeing body of a church or mission rather than to an individual?				
10. Is the program and money for the program from different sources, rather than both from a single outside source?				

4
Managing Accountability

Regardless of the type of ministry or its size, every partnership needs to maintain accountability. It is the foundation for safeguarding credibility and building trust. Partners with clear systems of accountability are better equipped to handle the inevitable mistakes and misunderstandings that occur in intercultural partnerships.

Certainly accountability is no panacea. It doesn't eliminate cross-cultural confusion, it doesn't do away with poor performance, and it doesn't overcome personality conflicts. But while accountability cannot ensure a trouble-free partnership, it can keep the relationship on an even keel.

Accountability is easy to understand, but it is difficult to implement. To use it effectively, partners must have a common commitment to it, a clear understanding of what they are accountable for, and a shared set of ground rules.

DEVELOP COMMITMENT TO ACCOUNTABILITY

There are three steps to developing a common commitment to accountability:

Check the way you think about accountability. Somehow we tend to think of it as a one-way street. Accountability is something we *get*, not something we *give*. Test yourself to see if you fall into this trap: What did you think of when you read the title to this chapter? Was your first thought, "This is about how to get the 'nationals' to be accountable"? Rarely have I heard someone ask how to make *him or herself* accountable to a partner ministry. It's always about how to make the other guy accountable. So the first principle is that accountability is a two-way street. This is the difference between partnership and paternalism.

Discuss accountability with your partners. The necessity of accountability is so widely recognized that we tend to assume that everyone understands it. To avoid this mistake, make it a subject of discussion early on in the partnership. Start by asking your partners what accountability means to them. Discuss how it works in their culture and how it works in yours. Work through the following questions together:

- What is the purpose of accountability?
- How is it usually practiced?
- What are the benefits of accountability?
- How is it abused?

Write a joint definition and purpose of accountability. After you have reached some mutual understanding, define accountability and state its purpose for the partnership. This exercise leads naturally into identifying what it is you will be accountable for.

IDENTIFY CONFIDENCE FACTORS

Confidence factors are qualities or conditions that give you confidence that your partners will be able to fulfill their responsibilities to the partnership. What essential qualities or characteristics give you confidence that the partnership is healthy and productive? What do you need to know that makes you feel good about the relationship? (It may help to put it in the negative: What would cause you to lose confidence in your partners? What conditions or behaviors would threaten the relationship?) Each partner should do this exercise independently, then share their lists.

At Partners International, we start with a list of six confidence factors developed by Alex Araujo.[1] Over the years we have learned that when a ministry has the following characteristics, we can have confidence that they will fulfill their commitment to the partnership.

A reliable accountability structure. Does the ministry have an accountability structure, such as a board of directors or the equivalent? Everyone needs to be under authority. Just as churches need elders, organizations need a board of governors who take seriously their responsibility to safeguard integrity, and steward resources, and to shepherd the leaders and staff of the ministry.

Clear goals. Does the ministry have clear, measurable, and achievable goals and objectives? In a small ministry where everyone knows intuitively what they have to accomplish and why, it's possible to operate without written goals and objectives. But the moment you introduce a foreign partner, that is no longer sufficient. Partners have to get specific, especially cross-cultural partners. Clear goals and objectives tell the partners what to do, when to do it, and how to measure progress.

Written policies. Does the ministry have written policies and procedures for managing money and personnel? This can sound bureaucratic, especially to a rural ministry in an oral society. It may also present problems in places where Christian activity is restricted or illegal. Still, we prefer to work with ministries that have fiscal policies and procedures. The policy does not have to be lengthy, but it does have to be formalized and the staff should be familiar with it.

Capable personnel. Does the partner have the right number of personnel with the right skills to carry out its plan? Ministries are notorious for overestimating what they can accomplish. And they attempt to compensate by working harder rather than smarter. The result is a chronically overworked staff, people in the wrong jobs, deterioration in work performance, and, eventually, burnout. Under these conditions the partnership may be at risk. A good partner has to have the courage to point this out and a willingness to help solve the problem.

A good reputation. Does the ministry have credibility among local Christians? If local people feel good about an organization, chances are you can too. But assessing a ministry's reputation cross-culturally can be tricky business. It's important to talk to several people who stand in different relationships to the ministry and to one another. At a minimum, this should include local and regional ministry leaders, companies with which the ministry does business, the board of directors and employees, and the constituents or people served by the ministry.

A favorable track record. Do they have a history of keeping their commitments? Ask your prospective partner for the names of clients, suppliers, and other ministries with whom they have worked for at least two or three years. Contact these clients and ask how the ministry has handled its commitments. Ask about the ministry's track record over a range of issues such as paying bills, meeting dead-lines, communicating with donors, and reporting results.

Other confidence factors might include fund-raising practices, publicity techniques, and financial self-reliance. Few areas raise more concerns than financial practices. In fact, it's fair to say that the entire issue of accountability is driven by suspicions about finances.[2] For example, suspicions arise when partners make unilateral decisions that affect the partnership. The problem with unilateral decisions is that the other partner may not be prepared to—or even desire to—follow through. When this happens, it is generally with respect to money. By offering aid, resource rich Western agencies can unwittingly become paternalistic. The receiving ministry may find it difficult to refuse because they don't want to embarrass the Western partner, or because they feel they really do need the money. Conversely, receiving agencies can obligate their funding partners by soliciting their partner's donors without prior agreement. You can avoid mistakes like these by conferring with your partners before you make any decision that might obligate them in some way. A confidence factor might well make a statement to this effect.

Once you've identified the confidence factors that make sense to you and your partners, you can move on to formulating ground rules.

Establish Ground Rules

Here are some ground rules to help you implement accountability. They are most appropriate for partnerships in which a foreign partner provides financial subsidy to a local ministry.

State your expectations in writing. To what will you hold one another accountable? Write it down. Whether you plan to use the six confidence factors above or a different list, put it in writing. Understand that this is not the same as insisting on a contract. The purpose is not to ensure compliance, but to avoid miscommunication and false assumptions. The problem with expectations is that they tend to change over time without our realizing it. If they are written out, however, we can always come back to that objective point of reference.

Share all relevant information. This rule requires that partners share all of the information they have that might affect the way they solve a problem or make a decision. Sharing ensures that all partners have the same data, including information that may reflect poorly on the partnership. (This means all information that pertains to the partnership, not necessarily all information about each ministry.)

Focus on outcomes, not intentions. For a ministry to navigate through the shifts and surprises of an ever-changing world, clear expectations are crucial. In the end, however, expectations are little more than good intentions. It's what actually happens as a result of ministry activity that is important. Accountability works best when each partner's performance is assessed on actual outcomes.

Review confidence factors often. The typical review process involves scheduling interviews to discuss where each ministry stands in relation to the confidence factors. Better partnerships meet annually. The best partnerships bring key personnel together twice a year. In any case, there is no substitute for face-to-face discussions about the issues that can make or break the relationship.

Resolve conflicts immediately. Partners working across cultural, economic, and geographical distances are bound to have conflicts. It's a given. It is unrealistic to attempt to keep conflicts from occurring. A better solution is to set up the relationship in such a way that disputes are resolved immediately. Immediacy is important because, when faced with a difficult problem, people tend to take the easy way out. Given the options of facing up to differences of opinion, resolving disputes, or avoiding conflict altogether, partners will likely choose avoidance unless they have agreed ahead of time to confront conflict and work through it to a resolution. It is surprisingly liberating to acknowledge that conflict is part of partnership, and that it can be used as a means of learning and growing.

For ground rules to be useful, everyone must understand them, agree on their meanings, and commit to using them. Partners should agree to use a specific set of ground rules only after they have carefully discussed them.

Once partners have agreed to follow ground rules, they must develop ways to ensure that they do so. One way is to refer to the ground rules when they review confidence factors and during other meetings. They might also critique themselves at the end of a review meeting to see how well they are using the ground rules and which ones they need to work on.

If you have worked out the ground rules in a negotiated manner, have not asked your partner to do something you are not willing to do, and consistently hold yourself to the rules, it shouldn't be difficult to get your partners to use them, too.

Twelve Ways to Be Accountable

You have heard it said that people don't listen to what you say; they watch what you do. One of the most powerful tools at your disposal is your example. What do your partners see in your accountability? How are you accountable to them and to other important stakeholders?

To evaluate your own accountability, ask yourself the following questions:

1. Am I accountable to an informed and involved board of directors?
2. Are my goals for the partnership clear, measurable, and achievable?
3. Am I as concerned about good results as I expect my partners to be?
4. Do I earn my partners' loyalty by giving them mine?
5. Can I be counted on to fulfill my promises?
6. When I ask my partners to incur some loss or give up a benefit, do I lead the way by taking at least as heavy a hit?
7. Am I diligent in reporting back to my donors?
8. Can local Christians say that I won't mislead my donors or feed them half-truths?
9. Can I properly account for my trusteeship of funds?
10. When I ask the partners for a financial report, am I ready to share mine with them?
11. Am I compassionate with partners in difficulty?
12. Do I ask my partners to tell me when they think I am off the mark? When they do, do I respond positively?

It can be difficult to jointly identify confidence factors and establish ground rules. Intercultural partners need a lot of time and discussions to develop appropriate accountability. Such shortcuts as mailing out surveys or evaluation forms do not make for effective accountability. On the contrary, espouse a relational approach that may involve more work than you expected. You are certain to find that the results are well worth the effort.

ACCOUNTABILITY CHECKLIST
Eight Steps to Manage Accountability

	Current Status			Action (When & Whom)
	Have it	Don't have it	Needs work	
1. Do we really know what we mean by accountability?				
2. Are we convinced that accountability works both ways?				
3. Do we understand what our partners mean by accountability?				
4. Do we have a joint statement on the purpose of accountability?				
5. Have we identified the confidence factors crucial to both partners?				
6. Do we have clear ground rules for managing accountability?				
7. Are the confidence factors reviewed at least annually?				
8. Do we walk the talk?				

5

Building Capacity

The decisive factor in a developmental partnership is managing the gray area between what *you* can do for a ministry and what *they* should do for themselves. The problem is knowing when to get involved and when to hold back, when to be supportive and when to be challenging. Here lies the tension between meeting needs and building capacity and self-sufficiency.

MEETING NEEDS

Meeting needs is not necessarily the same as facilitating development. It may be little more than undisciplined giving. "Acts of charity can be dangerous," John Perkins writes, "because givers can feel good about actions that actually accomplish very little, or even create dependency. Overcoming an attitude of charity is a difficult task because it requires givers to demand more of themselves than good will."[1] The first challenge to meeting needs is to "disconnect what and how we give from our need to feel good about ourselves."[2]

At best, need is a relative concept. The definition of need depends primarily upon those who undertake to mitigate the need. That's a problem for at least four reasons.

People with different values, and especially those with different cultural perspectives, will recognize different needs. The person *observing* the need and the person *experiencing* the need may differ in their ideas of what the need is. Consequently, the task of identifying and defining needs is not a straightforward process, but a negotiated task in which all partners are fully engaged.

Needs are not singular; they are diffuse and interrelated. For example, a school in Central America realized it could no longer grow past a certain point without a larger facility. That would mean a large increase in operating costs, which in turn would require substantial growth in local funding. But the school was closely associated with one local church. This precluded financial appeals to a wider Christian public. So the school had to seek autonomy from the local church. Thus, the perceived need was actually part of a cluster of needs.

Needs cannot be understood in isolation from their context. An understanding of the people and the environment is essential. The best way to understand needs is to work shoulder to shoulder with the people. By discovering your partner's needs together with them, and by making their needs your own, you can begin to help bring about real, lasting change.

Needs are dynamic. Because organizations are in a state of almost perpetual change, in a short time the needs that give rise to outside intervention may no longer be of the same magnitude. This alone is enough of a reason to maintain a relationship that is open and fluid, one that allows expectations to evolve with changing circumstances.

It's one thing to understand a need, but it is quite another to answer that need. At the very least, the ability to alleviate needs requires the following:

- *Before searching for solutions, it is important to understand the gap between the present situation and the result or end condition people want to create.* A gap analysis will allow you to determine whether a gap exists in a particular situation and then describe what is needed to fill it.

- *There must be a process for translating needs into organizational programs.* It's tough enough to plan and implement interventions in your own organization. Developmental partnering means working through this process with your overseas counterpart.

- *There must be sufficient resources.* Effective implementation comes down to the ability to reallocate existing resources, or to appropriate new ones. The more these resources are indigenous, the more lasting their impact.

If you help people define their own needs, search for solutions, and mobilize their own resources, then you will have begun the process of building capacity.

BUILDING CAPACITY

The key to building capacity is not in developing programs. It is in enabling people—the leaders and members of the partner ministry. Helping people learn and affect changes in their ministry is the most essential—and the most difficult—part of developmental partnering.

It is the most essential part because it releases the energies and creativity of people. It is the most difficult because people are responsible for their *own* development.

The outsider may help, but it is the insider who must do the work. This requires an interactive, negotiating style. It means that the outsider cannot presume to show the way; he may only help the insider to find it.

Whether we are dealing with individuals or entire organizations, building capacity has to do with being supportive of people in their own learning and development. The purpose is not to impose changes. It is to facilitate the process and to enhance the skills of people to implement their own solutions. Facilitating self-development skills is central to building capacity.

At a minimum, the skills of self-development involve the capacity to

- articulate needs, define obstacles, and visualize goals;
- seek new behaviors, skills, and technologies; and
- try them out.

Enabling people to work through this process is the heart of building capacity. To do so requires that we serve as facilitators, process guides, and resource persons. It requires us to support people in doing things themselves.

Here are six things you should know in order to successfully build capacity:

1. From the outset, leaders of the partner ministry must be fully involved in a process of discussion, investigation and analysis of perceived needs.

2. The entire process must be seen as a learning experience in identifying problems, and proposing and implementing their own solutions.

3. Facilitators must have a high regard for their partners' competencies.

4. All partners must view themselves as participants in a dialog between equals. They must remain open and willing to learn from one another.

5. Facilitators must be skilled at getting close enough to their partners to understand their situations and points of view.

6. Success is measured by the increased capability of the ministry to mobilize creative potential and indigenous resources.

Enhancing Self-sufficiency

Self-sufficiency begins by acknowledging the all-sufficiency of Christ. Only God is self-reliant. The rest of us must be God-reliant. To be self-sufficient does not mean to be independent of Christ or the rest of His body.

In this conception, "self" is not egoism. Rather, it is personal responsibility. "Sufficiency" is not independence, but having enough to meet one's needs on the basis of one's capabilities. A self-sufficient (or self-reliant) organization grows and develops on the basis of its own capabilities and needs.

Self-reliance, therefore, may not be confused with independence. Rather, it is the necessary condition for fellowship and collaboration with the larger Christian community. Every ministry relies on a wide array of resources, whether they are at the local, the national, or the international level. The precise location of those resources is less important than how they impact a ministry's selfhood and faithfulness to God.

Self-determination is the capacity of the ministry to make its own decisions and chart its own course. When aid is imposed, self-determination is violated. This is true whether the aid comes by coercion or by inexperience. A ministry may feel compelled to accept aid when it senses that refusal would jeopardize the relationship, especially where the funding partner provides a large portion of the ministry's total income. In such a relationship the funding partner holds the power of implicit veto.[3]

The implicit veto should not be confused with accountability. It is not unreasonable to expect the one who provides financial resources to have some influence over how those funds will be used. The apostle Paul saw to it that the funds from Macedonia were put to the purpose for which they were sent (2 Corinthians 8:16–24).

The tenuous differences between *offering* aid and *insisting on giving* aid are difficult to separate. But it is successfully identifying those subtle differences that safeguards self-determination and reinforces interdependence.

Interdependence *is the capacity to relate successfully to the wider Christian community, and to collaborate with other members of the body of Christ.*

Every ministry, whether church or parachurch, is part of a larger community of Christians. Fellowship and cooperation with local Christians creates a network of interdependencies and, thus, of accountabilities. When a ministry is funded primarily from an outside source, its loyalty may shift to that source. Under those conditions the ministry may become isolated and impervious to correction by local Christians.

Financial self-reliance *is a measure of internal to external funding.* As a rule of thumb, a ministry should have more income from sources in its on region than from external sources. The issue in self-reliance is not the amount of money supplied to a ministry, but the *proportion* of its income. A majority of support from within the region represents a healthy degree of interdependence.

Many opportunities, however, may be lost without substantial outside assistance. Ministry start-ups or major initiatives can quickly exceed the rule. Cross-cultural mission ventures almost always rely heavily on outside funding. How can we insure that a ministry will progress toward self-reliance where outside funding represents the majority of total income?

As a general rule, it helps to visualize external funding as a progression from more, to less in relation to the growth of internal funding. The diagram below illustrates this progression.

MINISTRY DEVELOPMENT MODEL

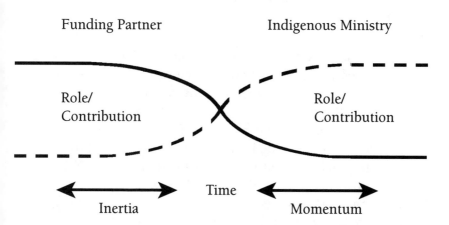

The model acknowledges that some situations call for substantial outside support. This helps overcome the *inertia* of initial obstacles to the ministry. In order to achieve *momentum,* however, inside funding must increase. The goal is to increase the ratio of internal to external funding. To accomplish this requires serious effort by both partners. At some point, the ratio of inside funding to outside funding should begin to increase. The first milestone is the point at which the lines cross, when inside funding surpasses outside funding. After that, it is a matter of keeping the momentum going and diminishing the impact of outside funding. Enabling the ministry to increase the ratio is an essential aspect of developmental partnering and the surest route to self-reliance.

Whether we are trying to improve the ratio or to safeguard self-reliance, the steps are basically the same:

Establish expectations at the outset and recalibrate them from time to time. In a joint effort, start with the end in mind and, working backwards, discuss the needed outcomes.

Monitor and review changes regularly. This should include frank discussions of what steps the partners are taking to increase local/regional funding and shrink reliance on outside funding.

Evaluate the impact on self-reliance and make decisions accordingly. There may come a time when outside funding should be cut back in order to motivate the ministry to work on internal funding. But to do so would represent a breakdown in the development process. Funding sources should be reluctant to force their partners to improve local funding by using their implicit veto. A better solution would be to agree on a gradual reduction of funding while simultaneously working with the ministry to cut costs, raise funds locally, or generate income through creative enterprise.

In the final analysis, as Kenneth Donald wrote, "The answer does not lie in any set policy. The answer lies in being sensitive to what the Holy Spirit says in any given situation. The initiative must always be with God, and in each situation we must take time out to listen to what he has to say."[4]

DEVELOPMENT CHECKLIST
Eleven Qualities that Help Build Capacity

	Current Status			Action (When & Whom)
	Have it	Don't have it	Needs work	
1. Do we separate our contributions from our need to feel good about ourselves?				
2. Do we understand the needs as our partners see them?				
3. Are we familiar with the context in which the needs exist?				
4. Do we understand the scope of the needs?				
5. Do we have the capacity to help meet the needs?				
6. Are we building our partners' capacity to do things themselves?				
7. Are we enabling our partners to maximize their own resources?				
8. Do the partners make their own decisions and chart their own course?				

	Current Status			Action (When & Whom)
	Have it	Don't have it	Needs work	
9. Are the partners well respected within the wider Christian community?				
10. Have we reviewed and justified the level of our financial contribution?				
11. Have we taken time with our partners to listen to God?				

6
Avoiding Pitfalls

Partnering in missions is like learning to walk. It's a process of catching yourself before you fall. Even when you've got the swing of it, there are plenty of things to trip you up. Partnering is complex, and it is prone to errors both in judgment and in practice. This chapter is designed to help you deal with errors by providing a guide to the most common mistakes made in intercultural partnerships. If you know where the pitfalls lie, you can more easily avoid them. For each mistake, we also suggest a remedy.

MISTAKE #1
Assuming You Think Alike

One of the quickest ways to get into trouble in a partnership is to assume others share your perceptions and expectations. I know. I made this mistake and it almost cost me a dear friend.

Several years back a close friend invited me to get involved in a ministry to slum dwellers on the outskirts of a major city.

It was and still is a fresh and exciting ministry. What started as weekly visits by a group of local Christians has become a thriving church with vocational programs for men and women, and health and educational programs for children.

When the ministry was still a dream, my friend outlined his plan. Because we had known each other for several years, we jumped into the partnership without making sure we were clear about our roles and expectations. It didn't seem necessary. After all, we were the best of friends. We held many values and perspectives in common. It seems that working through details would be an insult to our relationship. We trusted each other. That trust was all we needed—or so we thought.

By the time my friend was well into the ministry, it seemed to him that I wasn't holding up my end of the bargain. Don't get me wrong. It wasn't as though I had made promises I couldn't keep. I was doing what I said I would do. It's just that he expected a lot more from me.

Through several discussions, we were able to get the issues on the table and resolve them in a spirit of humility and brotherly love. It wasn't easy. There were mistakes on both sides. On my friend's part, he overestimated my availability to help build his ministry. Since we were close friends with a long history, he thought it only reasonable that I would be as committed to the dream as he was. He also overestimated my capability to provide crucial resources. That was an easy mistake to make. At the time I was successful in business and was directing a small nonprofit ministry in the United States. He could easily assume that I had ample resources at my fingertips.

On my part, I assumed my friend understood the nature of my ministry. I was involved in serving several organizations like his. I was simply not available to give all of my attention to a single ministry, even if it was directed by my best friend. I also let him down by not clarifying what I was capable of doing. Although it appeared to him that I could raise needed funds, my own ministry was being paid for out of my pocket and by a few faithful friends. We were not fundraisers, and we didn't wish to become a fundraising ministry. It took several candid discussions for my friend and I to restore our relationship. Real healing came over time as we adjusted our expectations to the realities.

Remedy:
Be explicit about your expectations and capabilities.

In order to be clear about your roles, you need to talk about them—not just once, but over and over again. Communicate to the point of over-communicating. How? Try this 7-point approach:

Use guidelines. What are the most essential things you need to know in order to succeed in the partnership? Outline those items, and agree that whatever else you might discuss, you'll always cover those critical factors.

Have regular discussions. Plan to talk monthly, bi-monthly, or quarterly about your responsibilities in the partnership.

Inform your partner quickly. Few things will insult your partner as much as first hearing important news that affects his partnership from the outside.

Ask for your partner's opinion. Your partner represents an important information base, especially on his region of the world. Treat him as a trusted advisor. This will win confidence and will open up opportunities for discussion.

Send short notes. Share with your partner such things as progress on joint projects, events in your organization, or personal milestones.

Invite bad news as well as good. Since this can be difficult in some cultures, the burden is on you to understand your partner's cultural style. Still, he needs to know that you can't work in a vacuum, and that you need to be made aware of a problem before it's too late.

Relax together. Spend casual time away from the ministry where you can allow conversation to become more intimate.

Mistake #2
Promising More Than You Can Deliver

You've probably heard stories of Christian tourists who promise the first one thousand dollars on the spot, and then leave the problem of raising the balance of a thirty-thousand-dollar project to their church back home. But making a promise you can't keep doesn't happen only to the novice. Experienced missionaries can also overestimate their abilities.

The grand prize of my work is helping a ministry achieve self-reliance. So when I came across a ministry that was ready-made for self-reliance, I jumped at the chance. The ministry was called the Promised Land, and that's exactly what it was—a large agricultural cooperative owned and operated by dozens of Christian families. It was well managed, productive, and showed great potential for profitability. It had every reason to succeed—except one. They needed cash to get through an unexpected misfortune.

Political scandals had locked up promised funds from the local government. On the promise of the government grants, the project had borrowed money for land and equipment. When I showed up, several months later, the grants had not come through and the loan payments were taking everything the cooperative could produce.

Rather than ask for grants, they asked us to help find investors. At the time I was in business and had a lot of business contacts. How hard could it be to find a few investors? Except for the debt, the project would be profitable. And it was just a matter of time before the government grants would come through.

What I didn't face up to was that I knew nothing about finding investors. I assumed one of my business friends knew how and would help me. Well, it didn't work out that way. My friends did help, but they weren't any better at it than I was. We didn't come up with a single investor. I had to face it. I had taken on a project for which I was not qualified.

Remedy:
Make sure to under promise and over deliver.

On the one hand, you should stick to what you do best. Take on only those projects that are within your grasp. On the other hand, I hesitate to give that advice because it would mean never stretching ourselves. I would rather try and fail than fail to try. The question is, how much damage will you cause if you don't succeed? That's probably a better indicator of whether or not you should accept the project. If the margin for success is slim, you can take one of three approaches:

1. Make your apology and back out.
2. Recommend someone else who is better suited to help.
3. Under promise what you think you can deliver.

If your capacity to do the job is limited, make sure your partner knows it, and encourage him to find other options. For example, the Promised Land project didn't rely on us alone. They could talk to anyone anywhere. In the end, our failure didn't hurt the ministry, but it didn't help them either.

MISTAKE #3
Taking to the Road Without a Map

It is normal for partnerships to start with ambiguity, misunderstandings, and disagreements. A partnership is necessarily untidy as people negotiate values and interests. It is not normal, however, when major misconceptions emerge late in the relationship. This happens generally for one of two reasons. Either the partners failed to clarify their goals for the partnership at the outset, or they neglected to review and recalibrate their goals along the way. The net effect is like going on a journey without a planned destination.

All ministries are engaged in to achieve results. That's the purpose of being in ministry. But too often Christians are inclined to think, "We can't operate with goals and objectives. That's for business, not ministry." Yet, when you ask people why they do what they do, they'll talk on and on about what they want to happen as a result of their ministry. Those hoped for results are as good as goals in any language.

A key to effective partnering is to make hoped for results explicit. In the absence of such goals, the results of partnering tend to be activities that keep everybody busy but rarely meet expectations. Any achievements are unstated, unplanned, and usually unknown.

Remedy:
Establish goals that make a difference.

Establish goals for the relationship as well as for ministry impact. Even when the partner ministry as a whole has clearly stated goals, the partnership must have goals as well. For instance, suppose you've decided to partner with a ministry that has a goal to plant churches among an unreached people group. By partnering with them, you've adopted the goal of church planting. The key result or impact goal of the partnership is to plant churches among the unreached group.

Other goals are also needed to hold the partnership to-gether and to keep it moving in the right direction. These serve as standards by which to make decisions, and as mile-stones to check direction. They also implicitly say what *not* to do. Adopting change comes easier in the service of mutually understood goals. Inevitable misunderstandings are directed away from individuals and toward the goals.

In partnering, merely stating your goals is not enough. They must be the kind of goals that make a difference. Goals that make a difference reflect the purpose of the partnership. They are feasible, challenging, and underline the larger sig-nificance of the ministry of the gospel. Goals that make a dif-ference define the impact the partnership can have that never could not have been achieved without it. They are the hoped for results that make partnering worthwhile.

MISTAKE #4
Underestimating Cultural Differences

Intercultural partnership success requires some under-standing of the worldview, ways of being, and interacting used by members of the partner ministry. Consider this illustra-tion from a recent article in the COMBIAM magazine, *ELLOS y nosotros*. It tells the story of a Mexican missionary to the Tarahumaras Indians of Mexico. The missionary lived among the people, preaching his heart out for years. He even worked side by side with them to support his family. Yet he never had a single convert. One Sunday after he had preached particu-larly well and he saw his audience nodding in agreement, he was sure some would make decisions. None did. That after-noon one of the men came to his house and said he was going to tell him something that no Tarahumaras had ever told an outsider. From many generations past, their fathers had kept repeating that they should never trust any outsider (non-Indian) who came offering something without cost. The missionary had been telling them that salvation is the free gift from God. They simply could not trust that offer.

Being Mexican and ministering to the Tarahumaras of Mexico, did the missionary assume too much? It's easy to underestimate cultural differences, especially where there are strong similarities.

For example, I worked for three years with a ministry in Hong Kong. Although the staff and leaders were Chinese, they were very Western. They wore suits and ties, carried cell phones, and conversed fluently in English. Still, their cultural heritage showed up in deeper matters, such as in their approach to authority, leadership, and managing relationships. To work with them successfully, it wasn't enough to be open-minded, accepting, and respectful. I also had to understand how they saw things and what was important to them.

Remedy:
Build intercultural understanding.

It is vital that we anticipate cultural issues. Not only does that mean understanding the host culture, it also means understanding your own culture. Being aware of how your own assumptions, values, and beliefs are culturally construed has as much, if not more, to do with intercultural effectiveness than having knowledge of the host culture.

There are three ways to build intercultural understanding, and all three are needed to reduce cross-cultural uncertainties.

Learn the culture. This includes knowledge of your own culture as well as the host culture. Unless you become aware of your own cultural frame of reference, you will not be able to understand why you react toward another culture in the way you do. Learning the host culture includes not only reading about general cultural patterns, but also observing and inquiring about what you see. By taking the role of a learner in the host culture, you'll also be winning friends and building relationships.

Build relationships. Genuine Christian ministry is inconceivable without meaningful relationships. Progress in building relationships comes through spending time with people, sharing your stories, exploring differences, and taking on tasks together. It is in building the relationship that you will encounter differences. When you do, discuss them face to face. In this way you will build trust and mutual understanding.

Understand yourself. Although it is often overlooked, people who understand their own social style and personal tendencies are better equipped to adjust to cultural differences. By understanding themselves, they are able to anticipate their own response to cultural differences. This allows them to manage stress and to take advantage of particular properties of the host culture.

In partnership, developing cultural awareness works both ways. Understanding your cultural differences is a mutual responsibility.

MISTAKE #5
Taking Shortcuts

I like to think I'm too smart for someone to play me for a fool. But it can happen, especially when I'm willing to take shortcuts.

They say con artists succeed because people are greedy. They know how greedy people behave and use it to their advantage. Con artists who prey on Christians take advantage of trust and benevolence. You can usually spot them, though, when you start checking references. The chances of being scammed by a certified con artist are slim. Even the most modest investigation sends them scurrying. Where you're more likely to get hoodwinked is by someone you know.

A number of years ago we began to assist a pair of local physicians in a very needy corner of the world. They ran a number of clinics as well as other projects for the poor. For years it was an impressive ministry. Let's face it, these doctors could have made a lot of money at home. Instead, they chose to serve the poor. To do that, they needed financial subsidy. They didn't ask for much, and besides, they were skillful at writing prayer letters and communicating with Western donors. As the years passed we made a few quick visits. But with other pressing problems to solve, it was easy to take shortcuts.

The physicians began to enjoy a higher standard of living. I suspect they grew into it, much like middle class families do in America. Lifestyle tends to rise to meet the income, and then to exceed it. In the absence of accountability, the missionaries found it easier and easier to spend on themselves rather than the ministry.

When we stopped taking shortcuts, the deceptions started to surface. First, they danced around travel agendas making it impossible to have any time with them. Then they commandeered the agenda, steering our site visit team away from points of interest. Finally, when we broke through the charade, the evidence of fraud was painfully obvious.

Remedy:
Develop evaluation procedures and use them.

Establish procedures for investigating new ministries and maintaining accountability with current partners. For example, look at a ministry through the following six lenses:

1. Study the priorities of the ministry and compare it to other Christian ministries in the area.

2. Look for agreement in basic theological positions.

3. Check out the ministry's reputation and relationship with local churches and other bodies of Christians.

4. Examine the ministry's financial situation and support base.

5. Identify specific goals and objectives of the ministry.

6. Analyze the structure and quality of the board of directors.

What you can learn about a ministry by looking at it through each of these lenses is useful to maintaining the relationship as well as qualifying a new ministry.

MISTAKE #6
Forgetting to Develop Self-reliance.

It is a mistake to underestimate the destructive potential of foreign aid. Relief and development agencies have struggled with it for years. It is no less a challenge in the support of national missionaries or indigenous movements. We must take great caution to ensure that the partners' self-reliance is not undermined.

Self-reliance has three interwoven qualities: organizational self-determination, relational interdependence, and financial independence. A self-reliant ministry is capable of making its own decisions, collaborating with the larger Christian community, and surviving on indigenous resources.

Self-reliance is undermined when one partner unilaterally interferes in the administration of the other, when a partner is handicapped in its relationship with local Christian bodies, or when one partner cannot survive without the other.

In complementary partnerships, where each partner comes to the relationship from a position of autonomy, issues of self-determination and interdependence are generally not a major problem. Effective complementary partnerships can only be achieved by truly independent organizations. The question of self-reliance comes with the flow of money. The greater the proportion of funding from a single source, the less self-reliant the organization becomes.

For example, one of our partners planted churches successfully for more than thirty years. During that time we steadily increased our support. The more churches were being established the more we approved grant requests. With no other goal than to plant churches, the partnership appeared to be achieving its purpose.

It wasn't until the partner ministry experienced a leadership change that we began to reassess our impact on them. Although our partner had succeeded in planting hundreds of churches, it had become dependent on outside resources. While we had achieved the main goal of the partnership, we had overlooked the importance of self-reliance.

Remedy:
Include self-reliance in your goals for the partnership.

A good rule of thumb is to provide a minority of the partner's total income. A ministry that receives most of its support from local sources usually represents a healthy level of interdependence. Admittedly this is not always possible. Start-up situations almost always turn these ratios around. Special situations or capital needs alter the ratio for a period of time. The point is to be aware of the impact and work purposefully toward a realistic target.

From time to time ask each other a series of questions:

1. In what way is the ministry stronger and more effective than when we entered into partnership?

2. What would happen if we were to dissolve the partnership today?

3. Would the partner be destroyed, crippled for life, or handicapped for a while?

4. What would it take for the partner to recover?

In the end, your goal is to enable the ministry so well that
they are capable of growth without your assistance.

MISTAKE #7
Running a Race with No End

The easiest mistake to make in a successful partnership is
to keep going with no end in site. Long-term partnerships
tend to make this mistake more than short-term, functional
partnerships. Short-term partnerships are by definition goal-
driven. When the goal is achieved the partnership is dissolved.
A good example is the consultative relationship. Consultants
and clients form a temporary partnership to solve problems,
make decisions, and plan for the future. The consultative relationship is ended when the project is completed.

Although long-term partnerships may start with a clear
picture of what is to be accomplished, over time the relationship tends to dominate. This is particularly true where the
ministry is successful.

Examples abound of partnerships that seem to outlive their
usefulness. Ministries led by gifted evangelists seem to be the
most common. One such partnership was recently dissolved
when the evangelist passed away. Although he was successful
as an evangelist in an extremely difficult and restricted country, he left no enduring ministry. The partnership, which had
lasted for some twenty years, was based strictly on one man's
personal capacity. His success as an evangelist kept the partnership alive though it operated with no end in site.

Remedy:
Have an exit plan before you start.

Nowadays it is a regular practice at Partners International to look at long standing relationships and ask, "So what? What are we really accomplishing?" When the answer is, "Not much that could not be accomplished without us," we start the process of graduation. That's a polite term for withdrawal. It usually involves a gradual reduction of financial subsidy. In some cases other types of assistance, such as consultancy, actually increase in an effort to help the ministry fulfill its mission without our financial investment.

WHAT HAVE WE LEARNED?

Perhaps we can boil this all down into three propositions. The secret to success in intercultural partnership is to:

1. Have a vision for the partnership and frame it in terms of achievable goals.

2. Cultivate trust by practicing respect and integrity in every detail.

3. Evaluate the relationship by measuring outcomes.

For example, if the vision is to reach an unreached people group, how many churches will have to be started? How will you know when a church is viable? How will you handle information sharing and joint problem solving? How will you keep your promises? How will you know when you have achieved your purpose?

For any partnership in mission, it is critical that we give attention to achieving results that match the expectations of our relationship.

Prevention Checklist
Fourteen Ways to Avoid Pitfalls

	Current Status			Action (When & Whom)
	Have it	Don't have it	Needs work	
1. Are theological beliefs and ministry priorities adequately compatible?				
2. Do we have a clear picture of what the partnership can achieve?				
3. Do we know what each partner must pay, in terms of costs and changes, to achieve the benefits of partnership?				
4. Do we have the resources and skills to keep our promises?				
5. Do we have meaningful goals for the partnership?				
6. Do we have clearly defined roles and responsibilities?				
7. Have we negotiated fundraising policies and procedures?				

	Current Status			Action (When & Whom)
	Have it	Don't have it	Needs work	
8. Do we have a communications plan for the partnership?				
9. Do we have a system in place to measure progress?				
10. Do we have a working knowledge of our partners' culture and ways of doing things?				
11. Do we understand how our cultural tendencies affect the partnership?				
12. Have we given enough attention to building interpersonal relationships?				
13. Do we have a way to resolve conflicts and disagreements?				
14. Do we know what steps to take to modify or discontinue the partnership?				

The Author

Daniel Rickett is Assistant Professor of Leadership in the *School of International Leadership and Development* at Eastern University, St. Davids, Pennsylvania, and Senior Advisor of *Partnership Development & Strategy* for Partners International, Spokane, Washington, USA. In addition to teaching, Daniel provides consultation and specialized services to Two-Thirds world missions. He has conducted program evaluations, facilitated intercultural partnerships, and guided organizational capacity building for over twenty-five years. He has served on the board of directors of six non-profit ministries in the USA, five of which he helped to create. Daniel is a graduate of Michigan State University (Ph.D., Adult and Continuing Education) and Wheaton College Graduate School through Daystar University, Nairobi, Kenya (M.A., Intercultural Communications).

Daniel is the author of *Making Your Partnership Work* (2002), co-editor of *Supporting Indigenous Ministries*, a Billy Graham Center Monograph (1997), and co-author with his wife Michele of *Ordinary Women: Developing a Faithwalk Worth Passing On* (2001).

Endnotes

Chapter 1
1.   G. Thompson Brown. "Rethinking Some Modern-Day Missionary Shibboleths." *Missiology*, January 1984, pp. 92–93.

Chapter 2
1.   Chuck Bennett and Glenn Schwartz, "Two Christian Leaders Discuss Dependency," *Mission Frontiers Bulletin*, (January–February 1997), p. 25.

Chapter 3
1.   Craig L. Blomberg, *Neither Poverty Nor Riches: A Biblical Theology of Material Possessions*, (Grand Rapids, MI: Eerdmans, 1999).
2.   See John Nevius, *Planting and Development of Missionary Churches*, rev., ed., (Phillipsburg, PA: Presbyterian and Reformed Publishing House, 1958). Roland Allen, *Missionary Methods: St. Paul's or Ours?* (London: World Dominion Press, 1930).
3.   Cooperacion Misionera Iberoamericana

Chapter 4
1.   See "Confidence Factors: Accountability in Christian Partnerships" by Alex Araujo in *Kingdom Partnerships for Synergy in Missions*, ed.

William D. Taylor, (South Pasadena, CA: William Carey Library, World Evangelical Fellowship Missions Commission, 1994), pp. 119–130.

2. See "Hindrances to Cooperation: The Suspicion about Finances," first published in *Co-operating in World Evangelization,* Lausanne Occasional Papers, no. 24, Wheaton, IL: Lausanne Committee for World Evangelization, 1983, and reprinted in *Supporting Indigenous Ministries,* eds. Daniel Rickett and Dotsey Welliver, (Wheaton, IL: Billy Graham Center, Wheaton College, 1997.)

Chapter 5

1. John M. Perkins, *Beyond Charity* (Grand Rapids, MI: Baker, 1993), p. 23.

2. Perkins, *Beyond Charity,* p. 28.

3. Charles R. Taber, "Structures and Strategies for Interdependence in World Mission," first published in Mission Focus: Current Issues, Wilbert R. Shenk, ed., (Scottdale, PA: Herald Press, 1980), and reprinted in Supporting Indigenous Ministries, eds. Daniel Rickett and Dotsey Welliver, (Wheaton, IL: Billy Graham Center, Wheaton College, 1997) p. 69.

4. Kenneth G. Donald, "What's Wrong with Foreign Money for National Pastors?" *Evangelical Missions Quarterly,* January, 1977, p. 25.

Further Reading

Bennett, Chuck, *God in the Corners: Personal Encounters Discovering God's Fingerprints in Remote Corners of our World.* San Jose, CA: Partners International, 1997.

Blomberg, C. L. *Neither Poverty Nor Riches: A Biblical Theology of Material Possessions*, Grand Rapids, MI: Eerdmans, 1999.

Bush, Luis and Lutz, Lorry, *Partnering in Ministry: The Direction of World Evangelism.* Downers Grove, IL: InterVarsity Press, 1990.

Chandler, Paul-Gordon, *God's Global Mosaic: What We Can Learn from Christians Around the World.* Downers Grove, IL: InterVarsity Press, 2000.

Finley, Allen and Lutz, Lorry, *The Family Tie.* Nashville, TN: Thomas Nelson Publishers, 1983.

Johnstone, P. *The Church is Bigger Than You Think*. Gerrards Cross, Great Britain: WEC, 1998.

Kraakevik, James and Welliver, Dotsey, eds. *Partners in the Gospel: The Strategic Role of Partnership in World Evangelization*. Wheaton, IL: Billy Graham Center, Wheaton College, 1991.

Lausanne Committee for World Evangelization. *Co-operating in World Evangelization*. Lausanne Occasional Papers, no. 24. Wheaton, IL: Lausanne Committee for World Evangelization, 1983.

Lundy, J. D., *We are the World: Globalization and the Changing Face of Missions*. Cumbrian, UK: O.M. Publishing, 1999.

Rickett, Daniel and Welliver, Dotsey, eds. *Supporting Indigenous Ministries: With Selected Readings*. Wheaton, IL: Billy Graham Center, Wheaton College, 1997.

Rickett, Daniel, *Making Your Partnership Work*. Enumclaw, WA: WinePress Publishing, 2002.

Taylor, William D. ed. *Kingdom Partnerships for Synergy in Missions*. South Pasadena, CA: William Carey Library, 1994.

Partners International

Partners International is a global ministry that works to create and grow communities of Christian witness in partnership with God's people in the least Christian regions of the world.

Since 1943, Partners International has initiated strategic partnerships with effective indigenous ministries that focus on starting churches where none exist. Working in the least economically developed countries and in areas restricted to Christian witness, our key approach is holistic witness (word and deed)—to alleviate human suffering and share the gospel.

For more information, please visit

www.partnersintl.org

or write to:

Partners International
1313 N. Atlantic Street, Suite 4000
Spokane, WA 99201.

(509) 343-4000
(800) 966-5515
Fax (509) 343-4015

To order additional copies of

UPDATED
BUILDING STRATEGIC
RELATIONSHIPS

Have your credit card ready and call

Toll free: (877) 421-READ (7323)

or send $9.95* each plus $4.95 S&H** to

WinePress Publishing
PO Box 428
Enumclaw, WA 98022

www.winepresspub.com

*WA residents, add 8.4% sales tax

**add $1.50 S&H for each additional book ordered